HOW ECONOMICS WORKS

BUDGETING

By Sandy Donovan

Lerner Publications Company
Minneapolis

Lerner Publications Company
A division of Lerner Publishing Group
241 First Avenue North
Minneapolis, MN 55401 U.S.A.

Website address: www.lernerbooks.com

Library of Congress Cataloging-in-Publication Data

Donovan, Sandra, 1967–
    Budgeting / by Sandy Donovan.
      p.   cm. — (How economics works)
    Includes bibliographical references and index.
    ISBN-13: 978-0-8225-2665-0 (lib. bdg. : alk. paper)
    ISBN-10: 0-8225-2665-4 (lib. bdg. : alk. paper)
    1. Children—Finance, Personal—Juvenile literature. 2. Finance, Personal—Juvenile literature. 3. Money—Juvenile literature. I. Title. II. Series.
    HG179.D635 2006
    332.024'055—dc22   2005014378

Manufactured in the United States of America
1 2 3 4 5 6 – DP – 11 10 09 08 07 06

TABLE OF CONTENTS

CHAPTER 1
WHAT IS A BUDGET?

This might just be your best birthday ever. You've had a great party with pizza and root beer—the world's finest foods in your opinion. You got that bike helmet you've been wanting for months, not to mention your favorite band's new CD. And to top it all off, you are holding fifty dollars in your hand—a gift from Grandma.

"I'm Rich, I'm Rich!"
That's right, fifty dollars—two crisp twenty-dollar bills and one ten. What will you do with fifty whole dollars?

Take all of your friends out for pizza? Buy more CDs? Wait a minute—you might be able to afford a new CD player with fifty dollars. Then you wouldn't have to share with your brother all the time.

Sounds simple, right? Grandma just gave you fifty dollars, so you can spend fifty dollars on anything you want. Before you know it, your mind is racing. You have so many choices when you have fifty dollars in your hand.

But there are trade-offs. If you take your friends out for pizza, you probably won't have enough money left over for new CDs. And if you buy new CDs, you probably won't be able to afford that new CD player.

BANK ON IT People have been using some form of money for more than ten thousand years. One of the first-known forms of money was cattle (cows), used by people in ancient Africa. People paid one another in cows because they were easy to count and easy to move. Cows were also valuable—both as a source of food and as a religious symbol.

It doesn't take you long to realize that you're not going to be able to buy everything you want with fifty dollars—even if it is more money than you have ever had before. In fact, it might seem like you could blow the whole fifty dollars in one day and still not be able to buy everything you want.

The fact is, very few people have enough money to buy everything they want. And if you spend all the money you have right away, you won't have money left over for the future. You won't have any money for next year's school trip or for an emergency or to donate to help other people.

With careful budgeting, you'll have some money to spend on fun items while still being able to meet your needs.

But by making smart choices, you can get the most out of whatever money you have. This is the time to step back and take a look at the big picture.

THE BIG PICTURE: EARNING AND SPENDING

Before you decide how to spend your windfall you need to focus on plans and choices. It's time to make a budget. A budget is a plan for earning, spending, and managing your money, both now and in the future.

A budget includes both the money you earn and the money

MONEY TALK Modern people use the term *windfall* to mean an unexpected gift of money. But in the 1400s, when the word was first used, it referred to good things that literally fell down with the wind—such as fresh fruit blown down from a tree.

you spend—money coming in and money going out. Think of all the money you take in: the allowance you get from your parents, payment for jobs such as mowing the grass, gifts such as the fifty dollars from your grandma. Money coming in is called income.

Then think of all the money that goes out: money you spend in stores, money you put into a bank, money you give away to help other people. Money going out is called expenses.

The key to budgeting is to make sure you have more money coming in than you have going out. After all, you'd quickly be broke if you spent every penny you earned. So to make your budget work, you need to add up the money you have coming in and then decide how you are going to spend it. If you budget carefully, you might even have money left over. In this way, budgeting allows you to buy the things you want today and still save for the things you want tomorrow.

VALUE ADDED

Allowances give kids practice saving, spending, and sharing their money. Some parents give kids a big allowance and ask them to use the money for big things, such as clothes and lunches. Other parents give only a small allowance, to be used for special purchases. Some parents don't give allowances at all. You and your parents can decide what system is best for your family.

BIG BUDGETS, SMALL BUDGETS

Individuals aren't the only budget makers in the world. All kinds of groups need to know how to spend money wisely. Families, businesses, schools, churches, temples, clubs, and governments all make budgets.

One of the biggest budgets in the world is the U.S. government's budget. It includes spending for military forces, schools, roads, public transportation, law courts, medical care, research, and public television and radio. It takes a staff of thousands of people to manage the U.S. government budget. State and city governments make budgets too. These budgets include money for police and fire departments as well as for schools, roads, and other public services.

TRACKING YOUR BUDGET

Some people keep track of their budgets in their heads

VALUE ADDED

The U.S. government budget is gigantic. In 2003 the U.S. government had approximately $1.8 trillion in income. Most of the income came from taxes paid by individuals and businesses. The same year, the U.S. government had approximately $2.2 trillion in expenses. So by doing the math, we can see that the U.S. government spent about $400 billion more than it took in that year. Many critics say that the U.S. government needs to do a better job of budgeting.

Many individuals (and businesses) use computer programs to help them with their budgets.

or on paper. Others like to use computers to make and balance their budgets. Lots of computer programs can help families and businesses make budgets. Most programs ask people to enter information about how much money they earn and spend. The computer helps them figure out what they can afford to buy and how much they need to save to reach their goals. The biggest businesses and governments use vast networks of computers to keep track of their income, expenses, and other budgeting categories.

CHAPTER 2
MONEY COMING IN

So you're ready to make a budget. The first thing you need is money. "Great," you say. "I'll go get some." But where do you get money?

Many kids get an allowance. Maybe your parents give you five dollars every Friday afternoon. That's five dollars you can count on each and every week. Other kids get money by doing chores or jobs around the house. Maybe on Sunday mornings you earn two dollars from your mom by collecting all the trash in the house and taking it outside. Or maybe on Tuesday afternoons, your neighbor pays you

What are some ways you can earn extra money? Ask your parents and neighbors if they have any jobs they'd like you to do. You might suggest pulling weeds out of someone's garden, mowing the lawn, shoveling snow, or cleaning up the garage.

five dollars to take her dog for a walk while she goes to the grocery store.

Sometimes you get money just for being you. That's why your grandma gave you fifty dollars for your birthday. And you may get other gifts of money on other holidays as well. Maybe your aunt always sends you five dollars in December, your parents give you ten dollars each New Year's Eve, and your other grandma sends five dollars every year. That adds up to twenty more dollars a year.

MAKE AN INCOME CHART

Wow, this money is really starting to add up. Each week you get an allowance of five dollars, plus you can earn another seven dollars. Then extra birthday or holiday money might come in. To keep track of this money, make a chart that shows your weekly income.

WEEKLY INCOME

Allowance: $5.00
Collecting trash: $2.00
Petsitting: $5.00
Weekly income total: $12.00

Make your own weekly income chart. Then multiply your weekly total by fifty-two. Add any extra gifts to determine your total yearly income.

That total income might not sound like a lot. But when you multiply $12 a week by fifty-two weeks in a year, that's $624 in regular income. Now add in $70 in birthday and other holiday gifts, and you've taken in $694 in one year.

KEEP YOUR EARNINGS SAFE

Almost seven hundred dollars. That's a lot of money to take in every year. Of course, you won't get it all at once. But if you keep up with your household chores and jobs for the neighbors, each week you can count on twelve dollars worth of income. With so much money coming in, it's important to decide where you are going to keep it. You might carry it around with you, keep it in a safe place in your room, or put it in a local bank. You have lots of choices.

Suppose you decide to carry all your money with you in a wallet. This way, you'll always have money on hand if you want to buy something. But carrying a lot of money also makes it very easy to spend a lot of money. You might buy something you think you *have* to have one day. Then the next day, when you are out of money, you might wish it hadn't been so easy to spend all that money.

Another problem with carrying around a lot of money is that you could lose it. Have you ever accidentally left your wallet or purse behind in a store or at school? Did someone find your wallet, contact you, and return the money? Or did you lose your money for good? No one likes to lose even a small amount of money.

DOLLARS & SENSE Ask your parents to give you your allowance in one-dollar bills. That way, it will be easier to divide up your money for spending, saving, and donating.

To keep their money safer, some people like to split up their money as soon as they get it. For instance, suppose you get ten dollars for mowing the neighbor's lawn. You might put half of it in your wallet and the other half in a safe place in your room. This way, you'll have a little spending money on hand and some saved for later.

IN THE BANK

When you were younger, you probably put coins into a piggy bank for safekeeping. But now that you're earning dollars, you might want an even safer place to keep your money. Opening a savings account at a bank is a great idea, although you'll need a parent's help to open an account. With a savings account, you can deposit (put in) as much money into the bank as you want. If you need the money, you can go to the bank and withdraw it (take it out).

Banks are safe places to keep money. For one thing, banks keep careful track of money and keep cash locked away in safes.

A bank can be a good place to keep your money. The bank holds more money than your piggy bank, and you'll earn interest on your deposits too!

In addition, the U.S. government insures, or protects, money that people keep in banks. That means that if your bank goes broke, you won't lose all your money. The government will give you your money back.

Best of all, banks actually pay you for leaving your money there. Here's how it works: When you deposit money in a bank, you are letting the bank use your money until you take it out again. Banks pay you a fee for allowing them to use your money. This fee is called interest.

Some banks pay a 3 percent interest rate on a savings account. This means that for every one dollar you deposit, the bank will pay you three cents a year. For every one hundred dollars, the bank will pay you three dollars a year. Three dollars doesn't sound like much. But people who have thousands of dollars in the bank can earn hundreds of dollars in interest every year. And the longer they leave their money in the bank, the more interest they earn.

Banks offer different kinds of savings accounts with different interest rates. If you decide to put your money into a savings account, shop around for a bank that pays a high interest rate.

BANK ON IT Collecting spare change is a great way to start saving. For one month, drop all your spare change into a jar. At the end of the month, you may be surprised at how much you've saved.

CHAPTER 3
SAVING FOR A RAINY DAY

Now that you have added up your total income, you are ready to look at the other side of your budget—expenses. That sounds like the fun part of the budget, right? After all, who doesn't like to spend money? But expenses involve more than just spending money at a store. It is important to save as well as to spend the money in your budget.

Saving means setting money aside for spending later. For instance, maybe you want to become a professional snowboarder someday. You'll need to pay for plenty of lessons

Hobbies such as snowboarding are expensive. By setting savings goals, you can more easily manage your expenses. You may want to buy a new snowboard or have to pay for unexpected needs, such as replacing a broken pair of goggles.

and equipment before you can begin earning any money as a snowboarder. If you put aside a little money now, it will be easier to pay for those things when you are older.

SET SOME GOALS

To get started on the savings part of your budget, make a list of your goals. Goals are things you would like to own or things you would like to accomplish in the future. You can divide your goals into three groups: short term, medium term, and long term.

Short-term goals are things you would like to do or items you would like to buy as soon as possible. If you save for these goals, you may be able to meet them in just a few weeks. For instance, suppose you want to buy a pair of cool sunglasses that costs $10. You could save your $5 allowance for two weeks in a row and then buy the sunglasses. Or you could set aside half of your allowance ($2.50 a week) for four weeks. After four weeks, you could buy the sunglasses and still have a little money left over each week.

Medium-term goals are goals you would like to accomplish in the next few months or year. Suppose you want to buy a birthday present for your best friend. You might not be able to afford a great gift the week before her birthday. But if you know her birthday is coming, you can plan and save for the gift ahead of time. You could put aside just fifty cents a week, and in six months, you'd have thirteen dollars. Then you can buy a nice present—and chances are you won't have even missed those fifty cents each week.

Long-term goals are usually bigger and more expensive than short-term and medium-term goals. For instance, perhaps the seventh-grade class at your school always takes a big camping trip in May. All the kids stay in cabins and spend the days hiking, learning to fish, and exploring the woods and river. The trip costs $200. Your parents say they will pay half the money—$100—but you will need to save the other $100. If you start saving in fifth grade, you will have two years to build up enough money for the trip. By saving $1 a week, you will have $104 in two years.

VALUE ADDED

A one-dollar bill in the United States lasts for an average of eighteen months. After that much time in circulation (passing from hand to hand), a bill is usually torn or dirty, so the government will replace it with a new bill.

YOUR SAVINGS PLAN

Once you identify your goals, you can figure out how much you need to save. Start by adding up the amounts you want to save each week for your short-term, medium-term, and long-term goals.

Let's see: $2.50 a week for the sunglasses, plus $.50 a week for your friend's birthday present, plus $1 a week for your seventh-grade trip. That adds up to $4 a week. Put these numbers into a savings chart like this one:

SAVINGS CHART

GOAL	WEEKLY SAVINGS	LENGTH OF TIME
Sunglasses ($10)	$2.50	1 month (4 weeks)
Birthday present ($13)	$ .50	6 months (26 weeks)
Camping trip ($100)	$1.00	Almost 2 years (100 weeks)
	TOTAL WEEKLY SAVINGS:	
	$4.00	

Follow the examples in this chapter and make your own savings chart. Remember to think about short-term, medium-term, and long-term goals.

Saving $4 a week may seem like a big chunk out of your budget. But when you think about the goals you can accomplish, that $4 isn't really so much. In one month, you'll have that new pair of sunglasses. Then you can either come up with a new goal for that $2.50

a week you were saving, or you can use the money for another part of your budget. Either way, in six months, you'll also have a great birthday present for your friend. And in two years, you will have enough money to go on your school camping trip.

You're ready to take action on your savings budget. Your first step is to decide where you will keep your savings. A secret spot in your room or a savings account at a local bank are two good choices. Once you've made your savings plan, the next time you receive your allowance or extra money from chores, begin to put your savings aside. Watch your money grow until you meet your goals.

OPENING A SAVINGS ACCOUNT

If you decide to open a bank account, you'll need a parent to help you. Visit some banks in your area in person or online to see what kind of accounts they offer and how much interest they pay. Some banks offer accounts for kids, with special passbooks for recording deposits and withdrawals. Be sure to ask about them. Some banks charge a fee if your balance—the amount of money in your account—drops below a certain amount. Make sure that you know all the rules of whatever account you choose.

VALUE ADDED

The world's first piggy banks were made in Europe in the 1300s. The banks were made of clay and were shaped like pigs because people viewed pigs as a kind of "bank" for food. When families had food scraps left over, they would feed them to their pigs. Then, once the pigs were fat from the food scraps, they could be eaten in times when food was scarce. Similarly, when families had a few extra coins, they could drop them in a clay piggy bank. Then they could smash open the bank when they needed money.

Once you find an account that's right for you, you'll need a parent to help you fill out the necessary forms. After you open the account, the bank will probably send you monthly statements. Statements are documents that show how much money you have in your account, how much interest you have earned, and how much money you have deposited and withdrawn that month.

CHAPTER 4
HELPING OTHERS
WITH YOUR MONEY

Let's review your budget so far. You have twelve dollars a week coming in. Going out in savings, you have a total of four dollars a week, which you put into a bank account or keep in your room. Well, twelve dollars coming in and four dollars going out leaves you with eight dollars a week to spend. That sounds pretty good, right?

But before you rush out to the store, stop and think. Do you want to spend all that money on just yourself?

Wouldn't it be nice to use some of that money to help others? Many kids who want to help others include donations in their budgets.

Donations are gifts of money to charities. Some charities help poor children, others help animals, and others protect the environment. By donating to a charity, you can help those who are less fortunate than you are. You can also help improve the world. And helping others will make you feel good too.

No one is required to donate money. The decision is up to you. You decide which groups you want to donate to. You also decide how much money you want to donate. That amount will become part of your budget.

VALUE ADDED

If your budget is too small for you to donate money, you can donate your time instead. Many groups need volunteers to help them accomplish their goals. You can look up a group that interests you in the phone book or on the Internet. Call to see if the group needs volunteers. You might volunteer to work at a museum, a hospital, or a food depot.

One way to help a charity and have fun is to participate in a walkathon. Participants go on a long walk for a certain cause, such as the fight against cancer or homelessness. Walkers ask friends and family members to pledge a certain amount of money, such as one dollar per mile walked. When the walk is over, participants give all the pledge money to the charity. Many young people like to take part in walkathons because it's rewarding to walk and work with others who share your goals and beliefs. Walkathons can also be festive events featuring music, T-shirts, and good food.

So Many Places to Give

If you decide to donate some of your money, your first step is to choose which charities will receive your donations. You may already have a favorite cause, such as helping animals. So you might want to donate money to a local animal shelter. Animal shelters rescue hurt and lost dogs and cats and help find them homes. Perhaps you'd like to help children or families in need. Some groups buy holiday presents for needy kids whose families can't afford to buy them.

VALUE ADDED

Around Christmastime, you might notice people dressed up like Santa Claus collecting money in big buckets *(left)*. The money goes to families who can't afford holiday celebrations. You might decide to drop some of your spare change into the bucket. Most people make this kind of donation without planning for it, so they don't include it in their budgets.

More than 700,000 charities operate in the United States, and thousands more operate around the world. These groups advertise their activities using websites, newsletters, and radio announcements. Look for a charity that shares your goals. Search the Internet or ask for your parents' help in finding a charity that you want to support. Many people prefer to give to charities that work close to home. In this way, people can feel pride in helping their local communities.

SO MANY WAYS TO GIVE

Once you decide what charity you want to give money to, then you must decide how much you want to donate. Some people donate a certain portion of their earnings to charity. For instance, you may want to give 10 percent of your weekly five-dollar allowance to the local animal shelter. That means you would set aside fifty cents a week from your income. After twenty weeks, you'd have ten dollars.

When you're ready to make your donation, you have several choices. You could give the ten dollars to your mom or dad, who could then write a ten-dollar check to the animal shelter. Then you could mail the check to the group's office. Some charities allow you to donate

Writing a check is like writing a promise to pay someone money. A person who receives a check can take it to a bank and get the amount of money written on the check from the check writer's bank account.

An animal shelter is just one of many options when choosing a charity to donate to.

money online, using a credit card. You'll need a parent to help you do that too. But you might prefer to go to the shelter and give your ten-dollar donation in person. This might be fun, because while you are there, you can look at the puppies or kittens at the shelter.

When you're young, you might not have a lot of money to donate to your favorite charities. But when you grow older and get a part- or full-time job, you can make donating a part of your regular routine. Here's how it works: Many companies offer a system called payroll giving. In this system, employees sign up to give a few dollars from each paycheck to charity. A worker might donate five dollars from each weekly paycheck to an environmental group, for instance. But the worker doesn't have to write five-dollar checks week after week. Instead, his or her company deducts the money from each paycheck and sends the donation automatically. Many people like payroll giving because it saves time and effort and makes it easy to support favorite charities. And if a company sends money to a charity automatically, the worker won't forget to make the donation or be tempted to spend the money on something else.

BOTTOM LINE Most people donate to charity because it makes them feel good to help others in need. But donating has other advantages. Large donations are sometimes tax deductible. In other words, people who make large donations to charity can pay less money to the government when it comes time to pay taxes.

CHAPTER 5
SPEND, SPEND, SPEND

Now that you've taken care of the saving and donating parts of your budget, you are ready to move on to the fun part—spending. Let's figure out how much money you have left to spend each week. First, add your weekly savings ($4) and donations ($.50). That's $4.50 a week. Subtract that amount from your total weekly earnings of $12. That leaves you $7.50 a week to spend.

Can you buy everything you want with $7.50 a week? Let's see. First, make a list of everything you want to buy in a week. Here's a sample to get you started:

WANTS LIST

Friday night DVD rental:	$3.00
Saturday afternoon swimming pool fee:	$1.00
Snacks at swimming pool:	$2.00
Saturday night DVD rental:	$3.00
Sunday afternoon arcade game tokens:	$5.00
Arcade snack and soda:	$2.00
Milk at lunch, Monday through Friday: $.25 a day, or	$1.25
Total:	$17.25

Make a list of your own weekly spending. Can you make your expenses match your income?

DO YOU NEED THAT OR JUST WANT IT?

So your budget gives you $7.50 a week to spend, and your weekly expenses add up to $17.25. What will you do?

The first thing to do is to separate your *needs* from your *wants*. Needs are things that people *have* to spend money on, such as housing and food. Your parents probably take care of most of your needs. They buy groceries for you and give you a place to live. But you do have one "needs" item on your spending list: milk at lunch. That is $1.25 a week that you *have* to spend. You can't get rid of milk from your list of expenses.

Next, take a look at your wants. Wants are things that you would like to have or do, but you don't really *need*

Food, clothing, and shelter are a person's three basic needs. It is important to budget for your needs before you budget for your wants.

them. DVDs, snacks, swimming, and arcade games are all wants. You have sixteen dollars worth of wants on your list.

YOUR SPENDING PLAN

The trick to making your spending budget work is to cut down your spending on wants. This idea may not sound like fun, but you can do it and still leave plenty of fun in your week.

Let's take a look at your list. What are you spending the most money on? The $6 on DVDs on Friday and

The arcade is lots of fun, but like anything else on your "wants" list, if you spend too much money on arcade games, you will soon go broke.

Saturday night. You can cut this amount in half by renting a DVD only on Saturday night and doing something for free, like playing a video game you already own, on Friday night. You're also spending $5 on arcade games every Sunday. But what if you went to the arcade every other week instead and spent only $3? And if you brought your own snacks to the swimming pool, you could save another $2. Finally, you can save another $1.25 of your Sunday arcade money if you decide to buy only soda instead of a snack.

With these adjustments, let's add up your new spending:

Saturday afternoon swimming pool fee:	$1.00
Saturday night DVD rental:	$3.00
Sunday afternoon arcade game tokens:	$1.50 ($3.00 every other week)
Arcade soda:	$.75
Milk at lunch, Monday through Friday:	$.25 a day, or $1.25
Total:	$7.50

You did it! You made your weekly spending equal your spending budget of $7.50. And you still get to go to the swimming pool and rent a DVD every week and play arcade games every other week.

WHAT'S MOST IMPORTANT?

Budgeting not only helps keep your spending down, it also helps you determine your priorities—what's most important to you. It forces you to ask: What's more important—that extra DVD rental or saving money for my seventh-grade camping trip? Would I rather buy snacks for myself or help lost dogs and cats at the shelter? Do I really *need* those new sunglasses, or do I just *want* them?

To figure out your priorities, in a notebook, keep a list of all the things you want to buy. You can add to the list every day, every week, or just any time you come across something you want. Then keep track of the things you do buy, the things you decide you can do without, and the things you decide to save for. After a month or two, look back at your earliest list. Do you still want all the things you wanted two months ago?

Keep this list for several months. You may notice yourself becoming better at not buying everything you want as soon as you see it. You might find that you end up having more money to buy the things you really want later. You'll also have more money with which to help others or take care of emergencies.

BUDGET

WEEKLY INCOME	WEEKLY EXPENSES
ALLOWANCE $6.00	SAVINGS $4.00
COLLECTING TRASH $2.00	DONATING $.50
PETSITTING $	SPENDING $7.50
TOTAL WEEKLY IN	LY EXPENSES $12.00

CHAPTER 6

YOUR COMPLETE BUDGET PLAN—AND HOW TO STICK TO IT

Congratulations! You have created a budget that lets you save, spend, and donate a part of your weekly earnings. And the best part is that you still have Grandma's fifty dollars. You can save that for a big goal, or you can divide it up to save, donate, and spend.

Now all you have to do is stick to your weekly plan. You must remember to set aside money for saving and donating every week. And you have to make sure your spending doesn't go over your budgeted amount. It's easy to

36

keep track of your income and expenses with a budget chart like this one:

Budget Chart

Weekly Income		Weekly Expenses	
Allowance	$ 5.00	Savings	$ 4.00
Collecting trash	$ 2.00	Donating	$ .50
Petsitting	$ 5.00	Spending	$ 7.50
Total weekly income:	$12.00	Total weekly expenses:	$12.00

Create you own budget chart. Remember to make spots for recording your weekly income, your savings amount, your donating amount, and your spending amount.

You will have lots of spending choices every day, and you'll have to make sure they fit into your budget. For instance, if your friends want to go out for ice cream on Friday, you'll probably want to go along. But you may have to use the money you would normally spend on your Saturday night DVD. This trade-off will keep your total spending amount at the $7.50 in your budget.

Sometimes it's hard to stick to your budget exactly. For example, you might have to make an emergency phone call for fifty cents that you didn't plan for in your budget. But if you spend too much one week, maybe you can save a little more the following week.

BUDGET TRAP: SPENDING MONEY THAT ISN'T YOURS

With a little determination, you should be able to stick to your budget. But one big budget danger can easily wreck all your planning. This danger is called borrowing. Sometimes, if you don't have enough money to buy or do something you want, you might ask to borrow money from a friend or parent.

At first, borrowing might seem like a good idea. You get the money you need to buy something you really want. But to be a good borrower, you will have to repay the money later on. It will have to come out of your future budget. If your weekly income already equals your weekly

expenses, where will you get extra money to repay borrowed money in the future?

A lot of adults use credit cards to borrow money. You probably know what credit cards are. Maybe your parents use them every day. Credit cards let you buy now and pay later. This is how it works: The credit card company agrees to pay your bill at a store or restaurant. Then you pay the credit card company later. But companies usually charge interest (a fee for borrowed money) for this service.

Lots of people use credit cards responsibly. They pay their credit card bills on time each month. But other people get into trouble when they borrow more than they can afford to pay later. They end up owing the credit card company a lot of money. They also owe the credit card company lots of interest. Their debt—the amount of money they owe—keeps piling up.

BANK ON IT In about 1200, people in England began using sticks to record money borrowed and owed. The borrower and lender would cut notches in a stick to represent the amount of money borrowed. Then they would split the stick down the middle. The person who owed the money would take one side as a reminder to repay the loan, and the person who had loaned the money kept the other side as a record of the loan.

DOLLARS & SENSE In addition to monthly interest charges, many credit card companies also charge people a yearly fee just to have a credit card.

KEEPING YOUR BUDGET ON TRACK

The best way to protect yourself from borrowing trouble is to not borrow at all. If you pay for all your wants and needs with money you have already earned, then you won't have to borrow money and repay loans. Remember, every time you borrow money, you have to figure out how you are going to repay it.

Remember that the money you earn and the money you spend have to equal each other to make a balanced budget. A balanced budget will allow you to buy the things you need today and to save for the things you need in the future. Follow the simple rules outlined in this book to help keep your budget on track:

1. **Keep track of your earnings.** When you know exactly what your income is, you can better plan your expenses.

2. **Plan for savings before you plan for spending.** Keeping a list of your short-term and long-term goals will help you decide how much money to save and how much to spend.

3. **Include regular donations to charity in your budget.** Lots of people choose to donate 10 percent of their total earnings to help others or the earth—and to make themselves feel good too!

4. **Figure out a spending plan each week.** By knowing in advance how much money you have to spend on different items and activities, you can make sure you don't miss out on something you've been looking forward to.

5. **Stay away from budget traps such as borrowing too much.** Remember, at some point, you'll have to repay any money that you borrow.

Having a good budget plan is the first step to having good money sense. A budget will help you to make smart choices about money every day. Most important, it will help you reach the big goals you have for later in your life.

Glossary

allowance: a sum of money parents regularly give to their children, usually weekly

budget: a plan that details how much money a person or business has to spend and how the money will be spent

charity: a group that raises money to help people in need or another cause

check: a written order directing a bank to pay a certain amount of money to a person or company from a bank account

debt: money owed to another person or business

deposit: to put money in a bank account

donate: to give money, items, or time to help others

expenses: money going out, including money used for saving, donating, and spending

income: money coming in, including allowance money, earnings, and gifts

interest: a fee that borrowers pay to lenders. Banks also pay interest to people who deposit money.

saving: setting aside money for a future use

BIBLIOGRAPHY

Books

Lawrence, Judy. *The Budget Kit.* Chicago: Dearborn Trade Publishing, 2004.

Nissenbaum, Martin. *Ernst & Young's Personal Financial Planning Guide.* New York: Wiley Publishing, 2004.

Scott, David L. *Guide to Personal Budgeting.* Old Saybrook, CT: Globe Pequot Press, 1995.

Toohey, Bill, and Mary Toohey. *The Average Family's Guide to Financial Freedom.* New York: John Wiley and Sons, 2000.

Tyson, Eric. *Personal Finance for Dummies.* New York: Wiley Publishing, 2003.

Websites

MoneyInstructor.com. 2005.
    http://www.moneyinstructor.com (June 9, 2005).

Personal Budgeting and Money Saving Tips. 2004.
    http://www.personal-budget-planning-saving-money.com (June 9, 2005).

SallieMae. 2005.
    http://www.salliemae.com (June 9, 2005).

FURTHER READING

Godfrey, Neale S. *Neale S. Godfrey's Ultimate Kids' Money Book.* New York: Simon and Schuster, 1998.

Heckman, Philip. *Saving Money.* Minneapolis: Lerner Publications Company, 2006.

Henderson, Kathy. *What Would We Do without You? A Guide to Volunteer Activities for Kids.* Whitehall, VA: Betterway Publications, 1990.

WEBSITES

Don't Buy It: Buying Smart
    http://www.pbskids.org/dontbuyit/buyingsmart
    Do ads influence kids too much? Go to this website to learn how to outsmart the advertisers and avoid spending too much money.

First Community's Kid Budget
> http://www.firstcommunity.com/kids/kidbudgt.htm
> You can practice making a budget at this website. The site also includes games and activities about budgeting.

Illinois State Treasurer's Office
> http://www.state.il.us/treas/Education/bas-L7.htm
> Go to this site for a lesson in how to budget your money smartly.

Kids Making Money
> http://www.kidsmoney.org
> At this website, you can learn about ways that kids can make money.

U.S. Treasury for Kids
> http://www.ustreas.gov/kids/
> Here you can find out all about U.S. money, including how and where it's made, how banks get it, and how to budget it.

SIGHTS TO VISIT

Fed Center, San Francisco, California
> http://www.frbsf.org/federalreserve/people/index.html#sf
> You'll learn about banking in the United States at this exhibit at the San Francisco branch of the Federal Reserve Bank.

National Numismatic Collection, Washington, D.C.
> http://americanhistory.si.edu/csr/cadnnc.htm
> You can check out more than 1.1 million pieces of paper money at this collection, which is part of the Smithsonian Institution.

U.S. Mint, Denver, Colorado
> http://www.financialhistory.org
> You can arrange to take a tour of the U.S. Mint's Denver site—the place where U.S. money is actually made—by contacting one of your state's U.S. senators or representatives.

ACTIVITIES

SAVE YOUR PENNIES

Think pennies are pretty useless? You might be surprised how much money you can collect just by saving pennies. Try starting a penny jar in your room. Find a big, empty jar and use it to store any pennies you come across, including pennies you get as change or ones you find on the sidewalk. (A lot of people care so little about pennies that they don't bother to pick them up when they drop them.) If you really want to go penny crazy, ask family members to donate their extra pennies to your jar.

The trick to collecting pennies is to try to forget about your collection. You're not going to collect a lot of money right away—after all, you'll need one hundred pennies to get just one dollar. So there's no need to count your pennies every week or even every month. Just throw them in your penny jar and forget them. Then, after about six months, add up your savings. If you've managed to put in twenty-five pennies a week, you'll have six dollars. Sure, it's not a fortune, but you just might find something fun to do with an unexpected six dollars.

THE POWER OF 72

If you put one hundred dollars in the bank at a 3 percent interest rate, how long would it take you to double your money? To find out, just divide the interest rate into 72, like this: $72 \div 3 = 24$. So it would take 24 years to turn your one hundred dollars into two hundred dollars.

What if you found a bank that would pay you a 5 percent interest rate? How long would it take you to double your one hundred dollars? What if the bank paid 8 percent interest? What if you wanted to double your money in six years? What interest rate would you need to get?

INDEX

ABOUT THE AUTHOR

Sandy Donovan has written many books for young readers including *The Channel Tunnel*, *How a Bill Becomes a Law*, and a biography of President James Buchanan. She lives in Minneapolis, Minnesota, with her husband and two sons.

PHOTO ACKNOWLEDGMENTS